Reincarnation and Christianity

Reincarnation and Christianity

Robert A. Morey

Bethany Fellowship INC.
MINNEAPOLIS, MINNESOTA 55438

Copyright © 1980
Robert A. Morey
All rights reserved

Published by Bethany Fellowship, Inc.
6820 Auto Club Road, Minneapolis, Minnesota 55438

Printed in the United States of America

Library of Congress Cataloging in Publication Data

Morey, Robert A. 1946-
   Reincarnation and Christianity.

   Bibliography: p.
   1. Christianity and reincarnation.   2. Reincarnation—Controversial literature.   3. Apologetics—20th century.   I. Title.
BR115.R4M67   291.2'37   80-24497
ISBN 0-87123-493-9

About the Author

Dr. Morey received a B.A. in philosophy from Covenant College, a M.Div. in theology and a D.Min. in cults from Westminster Theological Seminary. He is the East Coast representative of Witness, Inc. He is a frequent contributor to theological journals and has a regular ministry of conference speaking on Christian philosophy, apologetics, the cults and the occult. He is presently pastor of New Life Bible Church in Duncannon, Pennsylvania.

Dr. Morey has also written:

How to Answer a Jehovah's Witness
The Bible and Drug Abuse
The Dooyeweerdian Concept of the Word of God
A Christian's Handbook for Defending the Faith
Is Sunday the Christian Sabbath?
An Examination of Exclusive Psalmody
The Saving Work of Christ

Table of Contents

Introduction

In the last few years, various surveys have been taken by popular magazines to indicate what percentage of the American population believes in reincarnation. Some of these reports indicate that almost sixty percent of those surveyed believe in the possibility of reincarnation! Yet most Americans still consider themselves "Christians." Obviously, the Christian Church has miserably failed to indoctrinate its membership in the biblical view of life after death.

Since church members are not properly indoctrinated in Christian beliefs, the cults and the forces of the occult have flooded into this spiritual vacuum. Also, because the theory of reincarnation lends itself to sensationalism, during the last 75 years Hollywood and the supermarket tabloids have propagandized the nation while the Church has slept. It has become an "in thing" in Hollywood to remember one's "past lives"; stars excitedly describe their previous "reincarnations" on national talk shows. People flock to "self-realization" seminars where they supposedly regress into past lives through hypnosis. A flood of books and magazine articles exploit sensational stories of reincarnational recall which seem beyond scientific explanation or refutation.

Does the Christian Church have an answer to the theory of reincarnation, or should the Church lay aside its scriptural foundations and accept it? What about Edgar Cayce, Jeane

Dixon, and all the other so-called "Christian" reincarnationists? Can the Church defend its beliefs? Why has biblical Christianity been opposed to the theory of reincarnation? How and why did Christianity triumph over the theory of reincarnation in the first years of its existence?

This study is dedicated to answering these questions in the hope that many will rediscover the superiority of "the faith which was once for all delivered to the saints" (Jude 3).

Chapter 1

A Brief History of Reincarnation

The present popular Western concepts of reincarnation are actually refinements of the ancient theory of transmigration. This theory states that all human "souls" are involved in a cyclic series of rebirths in which the soul is eventually purged of evil by suffering, administered through the Law of Karma.

In the Indian *Vedas*, the word "Karma" originally meant "a sacrifice" or "a ritual act." In the *Upanishads* it evolved into the concept that any act in this life will have an effect on one's next life. Finally, in the *Bhagavad Gita*, Karma is viewed as a punishment in this life for evils done in the past life, with a prospect of purification for future lives.[1]

According to the Law of Karma, one's soul can be reborn into an insect, animal, or human body. For example, a gluttonous man could be reborn into a pig's body as punishment.

The Law of Karma is the immutable law that a person pays for evil he does in this life by suffering for it in the next life. If he is reborn as a worm or as a blind girl, this is his Karma. No one can pay his Karmic debt for him. All the suffering he experiences in this life is his own fault.[2] The Law of Karma will always catch up with him. There is no escape.

A person's soul, according to this doctrine, is eternal and is part of the "world soul" or "ultimate being" (sometimes called "God"). A person emanates out of this "cosmic energy" and passes through multiple cycles of rebirths until he is finally absorbed back into unconscious reality. One is "fallen" now because he is under the illusion of self-consciousness (I-am) and of subject-object relationships to the world (I-Thou and I-it). Through cyclic rebirths he will return to an impersonal nonconscious fusion with "ultimate reality." In other words, the person was *nothing*, is now in trouble because he *thinks* he is *something*, but will return to being *nothing* through Karmic cyclic rebirth.

The theory of transmigration was disseminated into the Western world in the form of Orphic mysticism.[3] Many Western pre-Socratic, and later Greek philosophers, held to Karmic transmigration in one form or the other. It became a firm Western as well as Eastern philosophic tenet.

With Eastern and Western philosophers embracing the theory of Karmic transmigration, it is remarkable that Judaism held to its revealed dogmas. Its doctrines of God, creation, sin, man, death, and salvation were contrary to the popular Eastern and Western philosophies. It is no wonder, therefore, that Judaism expended its main energy on survival and thus did not significantly influence the philosophic world.

In the world in which Christianity arose, most of the first-century Greek mystery religions, such as Gnosticism, held to various theories of Karmic transmigration. Christianity eventually displaced Karmic transmigration with its doctrine of Christ's substitutionary atonement in which He paid all of our "Karmic debt" through His own suffering. He had no Karma of His own, but He suffered and died for our sins.[4]

In the late 1800s, secularism, liberalism, and humanism began to displace Christianity through a rationalistic denial of supernaturalism. As Christianity was stripped of the miraculous and the supernatural, a spiritual vacuum was created in the hearts of many people. A revival of the occult religions, such as spiritism, thus ensued. Because secularization had stripped Christianity of its supernatural character, people began to return to the old forms of paganism.

Occult practices and theories grew because they satisfied the desire for the miraculous and the supernatural. Thus, witchcraft, astrology and spiritism began to gain acceptance.[5] The early part of the 20th century also witnessed a growth of occult groups which espoused reincarnation.

At present, many secularized "Christians" are gradually moving into the world of the occult. Since liberalism and neo-orthodoxy have fostered the secularization of Christianity in the mainline Protestant denominations, more nominal Christians will be drawn into the occult. Liberal theology creates the vacuum which the occult fills.

The theory of Karmic transmigration has been modified to suit the Western Christian mentality. Since a "Christian" would not accept rebirth into a bug or animal, the concept was redefined so that rebirth always took place in a human body.[6] This westernized form of transmigration was first expounded by occult groups such as Theosophy, and later by many of the Indian Hindu gurus who came to the United States. It was eventually adopted by such psychics as Jeane Dixon and Edgar Cayce.

Cayce, sometimes called "the sleeping prophet" because he gave his medical readings and prophecies while in a sleep-like trance, has done much to popularize this Western view of reincarnation. Cayce claimed to be a "Christian" who believed in reincarnation; but occult practices blended hand-in-glove with his reincarnation beliefs. He also accepted the basic metaphysical beliefs which formed the philosophic basis of reincarnation. Thus he was "Christian" in name but Hindu in belief.

The Western version of transmigration is, therefore, a "hybrid" of distinctly opposite religious philosophies, borrowing just enough of Christian doctrine to make it palatable to western minds. Because transmigrational thought infiltrated our society so gradually, few have noted what an inconsistent mixture it really is.

1. DeSmet, R., "A Copernican Reversal: The Gilakara's Reformulation of Karma," Phil. East & West, 1977, 27 (1): 53-63.

2. Gombrech, R., "Mind Transference in Sinhalese Buddhism: A Case Study of the Interaction Between Doctrine and Practice." History of Religion, 1971, II (2): 202-219.

3. Zeller, E., *Outlines of the History of Greek Philosophy*, Meridian Books, N.Y., 1967, pp. 31-35.
Dictionary of Philosophy, ed. Runis, Littlefield, Adams & Co., N.J., 1967, p. 221.

4. Machen, G., *The Origin of Paul's Religion*, Wm. B. Eerdman Pub. Co., Grand Rapids, 1965. In this work, Dr. Machen demonstrates that Christianity did not develop out of Greek mystery religions.

5. Cooper, S., *Reincarnation*, Theosophical Press, Wheaton, Ill., 1959, p.xii.

6. Cooper, ibid., p. 71.

Chapter 2

Four Popular Arguments for Reincarnation

ARGUMENT NUMBER ONE

"Reincarnation answers the problem of evil: why are people born with physical defects? why are people born into wealth or poverty? what determines the I.Q.'s of people? how do we explain where all the injustice, inequality and suffering in life come from? where do we get our personalities? The only answer is that people suffer in this life for the evil they did in past lives. The theory of Karmic reincarnation is the best explanation for all birth defects, physical handicaps, poverty, social injustices and suffering."

Examination of Argument

The theory of Karmic reincarnation does *not* solve the problem of evil. It does not even explain it. Most transmigrationists and Western reincarnationists believe that the human soul is eternal and was never created. Thus it never had a beginning or first life. To explain the problem of evil in this life, they point to its past life. To explain the suffering in that life, they point to another past life. *This method results in an infi-*

nite regression which only eternalizes the problem of evil without solving it.

On the other hand, if one postulates that there was a first life, this first life would have no Karmic debt from a past life to explain all the evil and suffering which it experienced. Thus, neither an endless regression nor a first life can demonstrate that Karmic reincarnation is the solution to the problem of evil.

The ancient philosophers used the theory of Karmic reincarnation to explain such things as birth defects, physical handicaps, low I.Q.'s, retardation, personality traits, etc., because they had no knowledge of genetics or the DNA code. They assumed that all babies should normally be born in perfect health and that all birth defects had a mystical or religious explanation, thus giving a mystical quality to an obviously genetic problem.

Recent studies show that the study of genetics in India is gradually undermining the Karmic explanation of birth defects. As mothers learn the importance of prenatal care, the number of birth defects is decreasing. Yet, prenatal care which prevents birth defects also puts Karmic reincarnationists into a dilemma. To admit that modern medicine can remove Karma or nullify its effects would deny that Karma is a "law."

Explaining the decreasing number of birth defects as increased "good Karma" avoids the obviously significant results of prenatal care—how can a scientific cure remove what is claimed to be a mystical Karmic problem? While we understand that the ancient reincarnationists did not have any scientific understanding of, or cure for, birth defects, modern reincarnationists have yet to refute genetic studies of the DNA code, or to deal with the studies' solid refutation of this classic argument for the theory of reincarnation.

Historical records reveal that reincarnationist societies have a sad history of neglecting prenatal care and proper medical care for those born with birth defects. Since physically and mentally handicapped people are supposedly receiving the Karma they deserve for the evil they did in their past life, they have been left to suffer in poverty and starvation.

Obviously, if the Law of Karma is right, we should not interfere with its administration of suffering. Is it any surprise that proper medical care for the physically and mentally handicapped never developed in Eastern countries which embraced reincarnation, and appeared only after Christian missionaries arrived?

The ethical question of whether one should interfere with another's Karmic suffering puts reincarnationists in another dilemma. If one follows Christian ethics, he must tamper with someone else's Karmic suffering. This dooms the sufferer to greater suffering in the next life because he did not undergo his prescribed Karmic suffering, thus hindering his purification and eventual absorption back into "being." Therefore, interference creates more evil and suffering for the person one attempts to help.

On the other hand, if the reincarnationist does not interfere and try to alleviate human suffering, his reincarnation belief becomes a source of evil. How can the reincarnational "solution" to the problem of evil be acceptable if it itself is a source of great evil?

As far as can be ascertained, not one of the Indian gurus who has made a financial fortune in the United States through Transcendental Meditation, Yoga, or his reincarnation beliefs has given one dime to alleviate human suffering. Where are their hospitals, nursing homes, special schools for the physically and mentally handicapped? Reincarnational philosophy cannot consistently support interference with, or alleviation of, someone else's Karmic suffering.

The only exceptions to this consistent application of reincarnational philosophy are the so-called "Christian" reincarnationists, such as Edgar Cayce. Their Christian background prevented them from ignoring human suffering. The reincarnationists from non-Christian cultures have generally neglected to alleviate human suffering.

Conclusion

The theory of Karmic reincarnation does not solve or explain the problem of evil. It has historically compounded the problem of evil by the belief that one should not interfere with the Karmic suffering of others, since all physical and mental defects are punishments for evils done in past lives. It has not engendered a compassionate zeal to alleviate human suffering. It can, therefore, neither explain nor alleviate the problem of suffering.

ARGUMENT NUMBER TWO

"The theory of reincarnation is true because many people have remembered, through various means, their past lives. First, most people experience *'intuitive recall'*—a feeling that one has seen the same thing before. Second, some children have experienced *'spontaneous recall'* of past lives—some of these cases have been scientifically verified. Third, many people have recalled past lives through *hypnosis*, having been hypnotically regressed to past lives under laboratory conditions. Fourth, there are instances of *psychic recall* through séances, mediums, or ESP experiments. It stands to reason that these people are remembering their past incarnations."

Examination of Argument

There are many obvious cases of fraud. Too many Indian gurus and Western reincarnationists have claimed that in one of their past lives they were Jesus, Moses, Buddha, etc. It is obvious that they could not *all* have been Jesus in a previous life! Even the most aggressive reincarnationists do not postulate multiple souls for Adam, Noah, Moses, Jesus, or Buddha. When a dozen religious leaders *all* claim to be the reincarnation of an important historical figure such as Jesus or Buddha, either they are all liars, or one is telling the truth and the rest are liars. Either way, most such claims are obviously fraudulent, regardless whether they were motivated by willful deceit or sincere delusion.

There are reasonable explanations for most other alleged recall experiences. *Intuitive recall* or *"déjà vu"* is that strange impression which comes upon an individual when meeting someone for the first time in which he feels that he has met the person before. A similar experience happens sometimes when entering a building, or seeing a certain location, for the first time. Reincarnationists argue that such sensations indicate that one actually met that person or visited that place before—*in a past life*. The theory of reincarnation explains these feelings as *intuitive recalls*.

There are several obvious psychological causes for these vague feelings. First, these feelings may arise as one's subconscious mind attempts to relate the present experience to things in his past: the person looks like someone he has known; the place looks like somewhere he has been. Thus he "feels" that he has met that person or was in that place before.

Secondly, one may once have seen a picture or photograph of that person or place. Although he cannot *consciously* remember seeing this, his *subconscious mind* accurately relates the encounter to the picture or photograph. Hence, he "feels" he has encountered that person or place before.

One man had such a "recall" experience while viewing, for the first time, a certain Swiss mountain. When he returned home, he discovered a postcard of that very same mountain. Although he did not consciously remember seeing the mountain before, his subconscious mind correlated it with the picture postcard, and he experienced an "I feel that I have been here before" sensation. His *intuitive recall* came from a post-card, not a past life.

Finally, this feeling often occurs when seeing people or buildings which are younger than the viewer. Since his present life extends well *before* these things, it is obvious that *he could not have met them or been there in a past life because these things did not yet exist*. Whatever else these feelings mean, we *know* that they have *nothing* to do with reincarnation.

What about *spontaneous recall*? Despite popular claims, the cases of children's recollections of supposed past lives *have not received true scientific verification*. Such a child's story is usually researched years, and sometimes decades, later. This is hardly scientific research. Usually, the child is already acquainted with the family with whom she or he claimed to have lived in a former life. Once such contact is made, no one is sure who said what, where, and when.

Nearly all of these cases take place in Hindu cultures.[8] This casts suspicion on their credibility, for why should *only* Hindu children recall their past lives? Is it possible that young minds trained to believe that they have lived before are encouraged to draw upon the richness of children's imaginations to fabricate such lives? Do not children all around the world *pretend* to be other people? When a reincarnationist's child pretends to be someone else, is he not encouraged to believe that he really *was* someone else in a past life? Such arguments for the validity of reincarnation are highly suspect.

While most cases of spontaneous recall are easily refuted by simply pointing out the unscientific manner in which they were researched, or the obvious psychological explanations of the experience, a few cases confound all reason and logic and do not yield to any rigorous critique. These stubborn cases will be dealt with later in this study.

Recalling past lives under *hypnosis* is perhaps the most popular argument given today. Controversy continues to split professional hypnotists. Yet, in the majority of cases, better explanations than the reincarnation option are available.

Many of us remember *The Search for Bridey Murphy*. After all the publicity diminished, the search was continued. Here was a woman who could speak Gaelic and talk about old Ireland while under hypnosis, but was unable to do either when awake. Researchers discovered that she had spent her earliest years in the care of her Gaelic-speaking Irish grandmother, who loved to read to her stories about old Ireland. Apparently, the woman learned these things from her grandmother, not during a past life. Though she consciously could not remember Gaelic and all the stories about old Ireland, her subconscious mind remembered and disclosed these things under hypnosis.[9]

How many other celebrated cases of reincarnational recall under hypnosis are, in reality, the unearthing of long-forgotten experiences and stories which were buried in the subconscious mind? The human mind records everything. The drawing up of these memories from the subconscious mind by hypnosis cannot *prove* reincarnation.

Several other psychological insights explain many of these cases. Many of those who recall "past lives" are actually talking about "*other lives*." These "other lives" are not past incarnations, but products of wishing and daydreaming.

Most people have daydreamed about the kind of life they wish they could live. For example, a certain man wished that he were a knight in King Arthur's court. His real life was so dull that he daydreamed, or fantasized, about himself in another life. This "other life" was not a result of actual experience as a knight, but a result of wishful imagination.

The man attended a self-realization seminar in which everyone was hypnotically regressed to his "past life." He regressed to his "other life" and thus described having been a knight in King Arthur's court. This "other life" fantasy was incorrectly interpreted to be the man's previous reincarnation. The reincarnationists assumed that if a person remembers either spontaneously, or under hypnosis, his "other life," he has lived a "past life." But, they have yet to prove that remembering "another life" is the same as remembering a "past life."

There are also cases of hypnotic recall that resist all explanation. These cases, too, will be dealt with later.

When we discuss occult recall, we must also examine the original means by which the theory of reincarnation was reintroduced into Western culture. The revival of the occult arts in the early part of this century gave reincarnation its present popularity. Witchcraft, astrology, Satan worship, and divination have, historically, accompanied reincarnational beliefs into the Western world. The leaders of reincarnational thought in the Western world *are* involved in the occult world. There are several reasons why this is true.

First, interest in the occult, including reincarnation, is rooted in the desire to obtain *supernatural power or knowledge* which is unobtainable through normal rational means. The attempt to open the door of one's past or future life is motivated by this desire.

Some reincarnationists are now saying that once you *know* your past life, you will have *power* to obtain health and wealth. Some even claim that all mental disorders are caused by incidents in a past life!

Secondly, a hypnotic trance is the exact mental state which *mediums* and *witches* have been self-inducing for centuries in order to open themselves up to spirit or demonic control. Hypnotic regression to a "past life" can easily be an occult experience. Thus, Edgar Cayce's readings were occult because they were given while he was in a self-induced trancelike sleep. Supernatural knowledge and power were communicated through Cayce while he was in his trance.

The same can be said of Jeane Dixon. She often "sees" predictions in her crystal ball or in astrological charts—ancient occult paraphernalia.

Thirdly, while much fraud is perpetrated in the world of the occult, the Scriptures never present occult practices as fraudulent. The Bible teaches that they are indeed *real*, but that occult involvement and phenomena are *evil*.

The Scriptures declare that God is *not* the source of the supernatural knowledge and power which can be obtained through occult practices. God strictly forbids His people to participate in any occult activities (Ex. 22:18; Lev. 19:31; 20:6, 27; Deut. 13:1-5; 18:9-14; Isa. 47:12-15; etc.).

The problem with modern secularized man is that he assumes that anything *real* is *good*. Thus he assumes that all spirits from "beyond" are good. He assumes that there is no Satan or that Satan is good. Thus there is no evil in the spiritual dimension. There is no danger in Ouija boards, séances, astrology, and reincarnation.

The occult is a game to many people. They do not realize *who* is the power behind the occult. This is a fatal mistake. If one admits the existence of evil in the *physical* dimension, does he have any grounds upon which to deny evil in the *spiritual* dimension?

Data from Scripture, history, and personal experience demonstrate that there *is* a Satan. He is a finite spirit being—i.e., a creature of pure energy not hindered by a physical body. Around him are gathered millions of other "energy-beings" who can kill, mutilate or possess the bodies and minds of human beings. This vast horde of extra-dimensional energy-beings constitute the forces behind occult phenomena.

Here lies the ultimate explanation for all those "unexplainable" recall cases. In every situation where a person recalled a "past life," and this life was researched and proven factual in even intimate details, and not fraudulent, the person was involved in occult practices. Supernatural knowledge was gained by contact with satanic beings. It is no wonder, therefore, that the theology which arose out of these occult experiences is exactly what the Bible describes as the "doctrines

of demons" or the "teachings of antichrist." Consider Edgar
Cayce, for example.

Cayce frequently spoke in the plural "us" and "we" when
giving his readings. Who were these individual people or spirits who spoke through him? Cayce himself wondered at times
if Satan was not speaking through him.[10] It appears that the
"us" and "we" who spoke through Cayce were demonic crea-
tures. Why?

The Apostle John writes in 1 John 4:1, "Beloved, do not
believe every spirit, but test the spirits to see whether they are
from God." He then gives two tests by which we can discern
the teachings of Antichrist.

First, the denial that Jesus Christ pre-existed His birth, or
that He was incarnate in a real human body, is of Antichrist:
"By this you know the Spirit of God: every spirit that con-
fesses that Jesus Christ has come in the flesh is from God; and
every spirit that does not confess Jesus is not from God; and
this is the spirit of the antichrist, of which you have heard that
it is coming, and now it is already in the world" (1 John 4:2-3).

Second, the denial that Jesus is *the* Christ is of antichrist:
"Who is the liar but the one who denies that Jesus is the
Christ? This is the antichrist, the one who denies the Father
and the Son. Whoever denies the Son does not have the
Father" (1 John 2:22-23).

Edgar Cayce fails both tests. He said, or rather "they" said
through him, "Christ is not a man. Jesus was the Man."[11]

Cayce's theology also does not accept Christ's bodily resurrection or return. According to Cayce, Jesus had already been
reincarnated thirty times and was probably absorbed back
into "being."[12]

Cayce also taught that "God" was an impersonal being;[13]
he rejected Christ's atoning work on the cross; and according
to him, the Bible was not trustworthy. He also denied the
Christian concepts of creation, heaven, hell, salvation, and
the Trinity.[14]

As to whether he was a "prophet of God," the Scriptures declare that God's prophets never make prophetic mistakes (Deut. 18:20-22).

Cayce prophesied that Hitler would be a good force,[15] that Atlantis would rise out of the sea around 1975,[16] and that mainland China whould be a democratic Christian country by 1968.[17] Only *false* prophets give *false* prophecies.

By biblical standards, Edgar Cayce was a prophet of occult forces and was not "Christian" in any legitimate sense of the word. His readings were supernaturally, but satanically, inspired.

The Apostle Paul warns:

> But the Spirit explicitly says that in later times some will fall away from the faith, paying attention to deceitful spirits and doctrines of demons, by means of the hypocrisy of liars seared in their own conscience as with a branding iron, men who forbid marriage and advocate abstaining from foods, which God has created to be gratefully shared in by those who believe and know the truth. (1 Tim. 4:1-3)

In the above passage, Paul warns of spirits who will seek to deceive believers into accepting doctrines which come from demons—i.e., from the extra-dimensional energy beings who make up the satanic host. Paul singles out two things which generally characterize demonic doctrines.

First, demonic doctrines will teach *asceticism*. Such doctrines teach that since all matter is evil and only "mind" is good, the body and its desires should therefore be denied. Abstinence from fleshly pleasures such as sex and marriage are therefore thought to enhance one's spiritual sensitivity. Paul refutes this practice in Col. 2:18, 20-23, and concludes that self-efforts "are of no value against fleshly indulgence." Paul therefore rejected the asceticism of the Gnostics, first-century reincarnationists.

The theories of Eastern transmigration and Western reincarnation have been characterized historically by asceticism.

Many of the new "mind" cults are openly ascetic in teaching and practice, thus confirming their doctrines as demonic.

Second, demonic doctrines will forbid the eating of certain foods, such as meat—as if such abstinence will assist spiritual progress. Eastern transmigrational philosophies practice ascetic vegetarianism and teach that the eating of meat is evil. For the transmigrationist, to eat insects or animals is to run the risk of eating somone who has been reborn into an insect or animal body as his Karma.

Western reincarnationists, generally, have also followed Eastern asceticism. But Eastern ascetic vegetarianism is redefined so that the prohibition of eating of meat is based on such vague clichés as "meat makes one violent and aggressive," or, "a vegetarian diet makes one at peace within oneself."

The Eastern concept that one could be eating his dear departed grandmother at McDonald's would not win many converts in the Western world. Thus, Eastern ascetic vegetarianism has been redesigned for the Western palate and lightly seasoned with religious and psychological terminology.

The evidence from occultic recall actually provides more material for *rejecting* reincarnation than for proving it. After all, since no one can return to the past to check out these stories firsthand, they are beyond *scientific* investigation. To the impartial observer, the "evidence" drawn from a person's supposed recall of a past life lacks any scientific or philosophic merit.

The arguments for reincarnation which are based on alleged recall point out a major defect in the theory of reincarnation: since the vast majority of people never recall any past life, or lives, they don't know *why* they are being punished with Karmic suffering in this life. This raises several crucial questions.

1. How is justice served if people have no knowledge of *why* they are being punished?

2. Since people don't know why they are being punished,

how can they avoid the same evil which originally caused the Karmic suffering?

3. If they don't know the evil which led to their suffering, are they not bound to *repeat* the evil?

4. Must people, therefore, keep making the same mistake life-after-life-after-life? How can they break out of this cycle if they do not *know* what evil to avoid?

5. Without any knowledge of the past, how is progress made or measured? Does it not seem that one is like a rabbit slowly turning on the spit of reincarnation while roasting in the fires of Karma?

It is doubtful that reincarnationists can satisfactorily answer the above questions. People's ignorance of "past lives" short-circuits any knowledge of or hope for the process of purification by Karmic cycles of rebirth.

There are also other problems. First, since virtually no one knows of his past lives, how can one know if this is his "last" life? If it is, should one "live it up" or deny himself in his last life?

Second, since one is involved in a cycle of rebirths and will be eventually absorbed back into "being," is there any real ethical pressure to live righteously in one's present life, seeing one always has another life to live?

Third, all the recall experiences we have examined omit any reference to anyone remembering when he was an orthodox Christian in a past life. This is astounding, as well as being an important observation.

If the theory of reincarnation is true, and its recall experiences are valid, then we should expect that when people are regressed into past lives through hypnosis or when they spontaneously remember a past life, they would recall all religious beliefs, regardless of their present beliefs. We should see cases of present-day reincarnationists who, when hypnotically regressed into past lives, remember being evangelical Christians. Thus we should find "readings" which proclaim that

Jesus is the Christ, that He is God manifested in the flesh, that Christ arose bodily from the dead, that the Creator is distinct from the creation, that reincarnation is a doctrine of demons, etc. Where are these Christian recalls? Where are the evangelical readings?

Suspicion is justifiable when *all* recalls and *all* readings espouse the same theological and philosophical beliefs. It is absurd to believe that all past lives recalled are only those of Eastern reincarnational belief! Why is there only one theology arising out of these occult experiences of recall?

The Christian knows why only one theology arises. Satan, the father of lies, began to espouse such beliefs in the Garden of Eden when he told Adam and Eve that they could become "like God" (Gen 3:5). Throughout history, Satan has continually baited people with this vain doctrine of the divinity of man. He is the antichrist who forever denies that Jesus is the Christ, the Son of God, the second person of the Trinity.

Conclusion

The argument using alleged recalls of past lives does not provide any valid evidence in support of transmigration or reincarnation.[18] Nearly all the cases are explainable on natural or psychological grounds, while the remainder are clearly occult experiences, fabricated by the forces of Satan.

ARGUMENT NUMBER THREE

"Christians should not be opposed to reincarnation because it was the original belief of the Jews, the Essenes, and the early church."[19]

Examination of Argument

Professor Hicks provides a masterful refutation of this argument:

Leslie Weatherhead erroneously and misleadingly asserts that reincarnation "was accepted by the early church for the first five hundred years of its existence. Only in A.D. 553 did the second Council of Constantinople reject it and only then by a narrow majority" (The Christian Agnostic, pp. 209-10). The fact is that reincarnation was taught within the gnostic movement from which the church early distinguished itself and then treated as a dangerous foe. We have an excellent example of gnostic literature in the coptic *Pistis Sophia*, in which reincarnation is in book I, ch. 7, and book III, ch. 125 (*Pistis Sophia,* pp. 8-10, 262-3). The first Christian reference to reincarnation is a passing remark by Justin Martyr, about the middle of the second century, against the idea of human souls passing into the bodies of animals (Dialogue with Trypho, 4-5). (Despite this, W. Lutoslawski lists Justin as a believer in reincarnation—Pre-existence and Reincarnation, p. 21). Irenaeus wrote his extended attack upon the Gnostics, *Against Heresies*, in the last quarter of the second century. In this he criticizes Carpocrates' doctrine of the transmigration of the soul, particularly on the ground that we have no memories of previous lives (book II, ch. 33). About the same time Clement of Alexandria made several brief references to the idea of reincarnation, which he did not accept (Stromata, IV, 12; VI 4). Hyppolytus, early in the third century, mentions again as a heretic the Gnostic, Carpocrates, and his teaching of reincarnation (*The Refutation of All Heresies*, book VII, ch. 20). The roots of Gnosticism were probably mainly in Jewish and Eastern rather than Greek religion philosophies; but at some stage the pythagorean and platonic teachings about reincarnation also entered into the debate and we find Tertullian, writing about A.D. 200, attacking both the platonic doctrine of the soul's pre-existence and the pythagorean doctrine of transmigration (*On the Soul*, chs. 23-4, 29-35). Shortly afterwards Minucius Felix ridiculed the idea of human souls passing into the bodies of animals (Octavius, 34); as also did Arnobius towards the end of the century (*Against the Heathen*, II, 16). In the third century the pythagorean doctrine was criticized by Lactantius (*The Divine Institutes*, book III, chs. 18-19). In the fourth century Gregory of Nyssa rejected both the pre-existence of the soul and "the fabulous doctrines of the heathen which they hold on the subject of successive incorporation" (*On the Making of Man,* chs. 29, 3). And in the fifth century Augustine attacked the notion of reincarnation in the course of controversy with the Platonists (*The City of God*, book X, ch. 30). All this means that the ideas of pre-existence and reincarnation were live issues within the early church; but it does not mean that reincarnation was at any time "accepted by the early church."

Again, it has been asserted (for example, by Weatherhead, *The Christian Agnostic*, p. 210) that Origen (c. 185-c. 254) taught a doctrine of reincarnation. The assertion seems to be based upon a misreading of the texts. Origen affirms the pre-existence of the soul and regards the fortunate and unfortunate circumstances of birth—for example, as healthy or deformed—as rewards and punishments for virtue and sin in the soul's previous existence (On First Principles, book II, chs. 9, 6-8). To this extent his teaching is in agreement with the idea of reincarnation. However, this previous existence was not on earth but in the heavens, and did not constitute one of a series of former lives. Origen does not speak of successive incarnations of the soul in different earthly bodies but only of the soul's pre-existence in some higher realm prior to its descent into this world. Indeed, in at least one passage Origen explicitly repudiates a form of reincarnation doctrine. Discussing Celsus' speculation about human souls entering animal bodies, he says, "Christians, however, will not yield their assent to such opinions: for they have been instructed before now that the human soul was created in the image of God; and they see that it is impossible for a nature fashioned in the divine image to have its (original) features altogether obliterated, and to assume others, formed after I know not what likeness of irrational animals" (*Against Celsus*, book IV, 83). Origen's doctrine of pre-existence, as well as a number of his other teachings, were matters of spasmodic debate in the church during the fourth, fifth, and sixth centuries, and Origen or his ideas were condemned by Synods in 400 and 403 (J. F. Bethune-Baker, *An Introduction to the Early History of Christian Doctrine*, p. 153). Either the "Home Synod" held at Constantinople in 543 or the second Council of Constantinople in 553—scholars dispute as to which it was—adopted fifteen anathemas against Origen, none of which mentions reincarnation but the first of which reads, "If anyone asserts the fabulous pre-existence of souls, and shall assert the monstrous restoration (apocatastasis) which follows from it: let him be anathema" (*The Nicene and Post-Nicene Fathers*, Series Two, vol. XIV, p. 318).

That Origen did not teach reincarnation is argued by Charles Bigg, *The Christian Platonists of Alexandria*, pp. 198f.; Jean Daniélou, *Origen,* pp. 249-50; and Jaroslav Pelikan, *The Shape of Death*, pp. 9 ff.

Origen's works were first printed in the fifteenth and sixteenth centuries and influenced the seventeenth-century Cambridge Platonists, and towards the end of that century some minor figures within this movement taught "metempsychosis." See D. P. Walker, *The Decline of Hell*, pp. 137-46.

For a survey of the patristic references to reincarnation see Louis Bukowski, SJ, "Le reincarnation selon les Pères de l'Eglise," in *Gregorianum*, vol. IX (1928), pp. 65-91.

It has been said, again by Leslie Weatherhead, that "one prominent sect, the Essenes, definitely taught it (i.e., reincarnation), and Josephus makes reference to it as if it were commonly accepted" (*The Christian Agnostic*, p. 209). He is referring to Josephus' *Jewish Wars*, book II, ch. 8, para. 14. This reads, "(It is said that) on the one hand all souls are immortal, but on the other hand those of good men only are changed into another body (metabainein eis heteron soma) but those of evil men are subject to eternal punishment." However, there is nothing here to indicate that the change into another body is reincarnation, i.e. being born again as a baby on earth. It seems more likely that Josephus had in mind the resurrection of the body, but perhaps (as in the thought of St. Paul) in another, "spiritual" body. Such an idea is found in Jewish apocalyptic writings (e.g., 2 Anoch 8:5:65: 10; 2 Esdras 2:39, 45): See D. S. Russell, *The Method and Message of Jewish Apocalyptic*, pp. 376-9.[20]

Conclusion

Too often reincarnationists dogmatically assert that the theory of reincarnation was the original faith of Jews, Christians, and Essenes. But the historical evidence stands against such dogmaticism. The reincarnationists must be careful to avoid rewriting history to suit their prejudices. This is why church historians do not support their claims.

ARGUMENT NUMBER FOUR

"The Bible teaches reincarnation. Wasn't John the Baptist a reincarnation of Elijah the prophet? (Matt. 11:14; Mark 8:11-13). Wasn't Melchizedek a previous reincarnation of Jesus? (Heb. 7:2-3). Didn't Jesus talk about reincarnation when He told Nicodemus that he must be 'born again'? (John 3:3). Didn't the Apostles rightly invoke the Law of Karma to explain the man born blind? (John 9:2)."

Examination of Argument

Objective exegeses of the above passages in their respective contexts will not uncover any reference to the theory of reincarnation or Karma. No trained exegete takes the reincarnationist's claims seriously for the following reasons.

1. *It is irrefutably clear that John the Baptist was not a reincarnation of Elijah.*

   a. Elijah, like Enoch, never died but was translated to heaven without ever tasting death (2 Kings 2:11; c.f., Heb. 11:5).

   b. Elijah showed himself still alive and in his original body on the Mount of Transfiguration (Luke 9:30-33).

   c. John 1:21 records that when the priests and Levites asked John the Baptist, "What then? Are you Elijah?", he answered, "I am not."

   d. How do we explain Matt. 11:14 and Mark 9:11-13? If we use scripture to interpret scripture, Jesus was simply saying that the *ministry* of John the Baptist was "in the spirit and power" of Elijah's ministry (Luke 1:17).

2. Melchizedek was a historical figure about whom there is little biblical information. When Heb. 7:3 tells us he was "without father, without mother, without genealogy, having neither beginning of days nor end of life," it simply means that we do not have a *record* of his birth or death—not even of his ancestry. He is chosen as a type of Christ because the priesthood which Melchizedek possessed was uniquely his own and was not passed on to anyone else. This passage deals with a comparison of priesthoods. It has nothing to do with reincarnations.

3. Only the most superficial reading of John 3:1-16 could support the theory of reincarnation. The "new birth" is pointed out by Christ as *not* being a "flesh" birth but an act of the Holy Spirit (v. 6). It clearly involves personal faith in Christ (v. 16). Even John 1:12-13 points to receiving Christ as the means of becoming "children of God." Thus, according to the

New Testament, the new birth is a *spiritual* experience, known as conversion, or regeneration. It takes place in *this* life and not in a life to come.

4. Instead of proving the Law of Karma, John 9:2-3 actually proves that Christ denied it in principle.

The Law of Karma would say that the man born blind had sinned in his previous life and was now suffering for his evil acts. Thus one should not seek to alleviate his suffering as this would interfere with his Karmic debt and only prolong his cyclic rebirths.

But Jesus flatly denied that this man's blindness had any relationship to his sins (v. 2). "It was in order that the works of God might be displayed" that this man was born blind (v. 3). Then Jesus healed him. In response, the man worshiped the Lord Jesus (v. 38). Nothing in this story could possibly support the theory of reincarnation.

Conclusion

The Scriptures do not teach the theory of reincarnation, or the Law of Karma, no matter how hard some try to read it into the text. The Word of God stands opposed to the theory of reincarnation. The reincarnationists must be careful to observe Peter's warning:

> And regard the patience of our Lord to be salvation; just as also our beloved brother Paul, according to the wisdom given him, wrote to you, as also in all his letters, speaking in them of these things, in which are some things hard to understand, which the untaught and unstable distort, as they do also the rest of the Scriptures, to their own destruction. (2 Pet. 3:15-16)

---

7. See *Religion*, 4:47-58, Spr. 1974, for a survey of the impact of genetics on reincarnation beliefs among educated Indians.

8. Hicks, J., *Death & Eternal Life*, Harper & Row, N.Y., 1976, p. 375.

9. Martin, Walter R., "The Riddle of Reincarnation," One Way Library.

10. Bjornstad, J., *Twentieth Century Prophecy: Jeane Dixon and Edgar Cayce*, Bethany Fellowship, Inc., 1969, p. 14.

11. Langley, N., *Edgar Cayce on Reincarnation*, Castle Books, N.Y., 1967, p. 157.

12. Swihart, P., *Reincarnation, Edgar Cayce and the Bible*, I.V.P., Ill., 1977, p. 18.

13. Readings: 254-34.

14. Swihart, ibid., pp. 12-20.

15. Ibid., p. 30.

16. Readings: 3209-2.

17. Readings: 3111-8.

18. According to the school of Advaita Vedanta, "Karma" is incapable of any scientific verification or demonstration. It is a fiction. See: Deutsch, E., "Karma as a 'Convenient Fiction': In the Advaita Vedanta"; Phil. East & West, 1965, 15:3-12 (No. 1).

19. Weatherhead, L. D., *The Case for Reincarnation*, M. C. Pero., Surrey, England, 1958, pp. 35-45.

20. Hicks, ibid., pp. 392-394, 395.

Chapter 3

The Intellectual Integrity of Reincarnation

The following is a summary of several more observations which cast serious doubt on Eastern and Western theories of reincarnation.

World Population Growth

The ancient philosophers had no way of measuring the world's population. Because of this, they made the following assumptions:

1. The world's population is basically stable—"As one dies, another is born to take his place."

2. Even when war or natural disaster reduce the population in a given location, other places experience prosperity and population growth. Thus, overall, the world's population remains stable.

3. There will, therefore, always be enough souls to be born into all infant bodies, for there is a corresponding number of deaths and births.

4. The human soul is not created but is eternal. Thus, no new souls are being created to enter the cycle of rebirths (modern reincarnationists also hold to this concept, e.g., Edgar Cayce).

5. When a soul is sufficiently purified, it is absorbed back into "being."

Because of these basic presuppositions, several serious problems arise which threaten the credibility of the theory of reincarnation.

First, if no *new* souls are being created and the number of *old* souls is continually decreasing as these souls are being absorbed back into "being," the world's population should be decreasing. Logically, there should be fewer souls in the cycle of reincarnation today than were in the cycle a thousand years ago. But this is not true. There are more people alive in this present generation than in any previous generation. Reincarnationists have yet to answer this problem.

Second, since the world's population is increasing so rapidly that more people are alive now than have ever existed previously, it is only obvious that there are no longer enough souls to match the number of births.

Third, the ancients experienced high infant mortality rates and low life expectancies. To them, it appeared that enough people died to provide adequate souls for all births. Thus, the ancient reincarnationists never had to come up with an answer to the problem of not having enough souls to go around.

Fourth, since they had already committed themselves to the view that souls are eternal and not created, and thus denying that new souls are being created to replace old souls, a *human* source for all the new souls required by the world's population explosion is out of the question.

Fifth, some Eastern transmigrationists have developed an answer to this perplexing problem. Since the total number of souls could include all the insects and animals of this world as well as all human beings, the present world population is the result of more human rebirths and fewer insect and animal rebirths. Thus, the needed souls are simply shifted over from the bodies of insects and animals to those of humans. This leads us to ask, "Why should the Law of Karma change? Why more human, and fewer insect and animal rebirths?" Their "answer" seems, on the surface, hastily put together without considering how it affects the "law" character of Karma. To admit that Karma has *changed* means that it is not a *law*.

Sixth, while the animal and insect solution is "possible," it still does not answer the problem of how and why the world's population is increasing. It is also obvious that the animal and insect solution still leaves many questions unresolved. For example, why are there more *human* rebirths *now* than before? Does *increasing human rebirths* really mean *decreasing insect and animal rebirths*? Why or why not? What has caused Karma to change?

Western reincarnationists are in an even greater dilemma when confronted by the problem of the increasing world population. Many Western reincarnationists do not hold to the transmigration of souls from animal bodies to human bodies or from human bodies to animal bodies. According to them, human souls are only reborn into *human bodies*. Thus, the Eastern animal or insect solution to the problem is not a possible option for these Western reincarnationists.

At the same time, most, if not all, Western reincarnationists hold to the Eastern concept that all souls are eternal. Thus there are no new souls entering the cycle of reincarnation. It would seem, therefore, that the Western reincarnationists have no room in their theory to secure the needed souls to explain the world's increasing population. They cannot turn to the past, to insects or animals, or even to new souls being created.

This is an insurmountable difficulty because it was never envisioned by the ancient or early Western reincarnationists. They assumed that there would always be enough deaths to explain all births. But due to modern long-life expectancies and low infant mortality rates, not enough people die to provide the number of souls needed for all those born. More people are born than die at the present time. This stark reality poses a tremendous threat to the credibility of the theory of reincarnation. The theory is self-refuting because it contains within itself the seeds of its own destruction.

Western reincarnationists cannot satisfactorily account for the increasing world population without rejecting or modifying some of their central and essential beliefs. This leads to another problem.

Man's Moral Condition

Since every soul is progressively purified and purged of evil through cyclic rebirth and Karmic suffering, it is only logical that we should be able to observe *mankind as a whole becoming better and better.* If all souls are individually being purified from evil, then *the race as a whole* should show some evidence of moral progress.

Since reincarnation and Karma have supposedly been at work for thousands of years, surely there must be some historical evidence of mankind's improvement. But is there any such evidence? Has mankind progressively and increasingly become moral, i.e., purified from evil? Has each generation been morally superior to the previous generation?

The obvious fact which confronts every Western and Eastern reincarnationist is that humanity is just as wicked today as it ever was. Mankind as a whole does not show *any* evidence that *any* moral progress has been made.

The reincarnationists could possibly reply, "All moral progress takes place on an invisible spiritual plane and there will be no evidence of it in the visible realm." But this answer compounds the problem. After all, why should men be punished in *this* realm for progress to be made in some *other* realm? How is it *just* that all our suffering in *this* realm of life (as we know it) *does not help* us in this realm? Of what profit is it if all progress takes place in some unseen spiritual realm? Why doesn't all punishment take place in that invisible spiritual realm seeing that is where the progress is made?

The only conclusion we can come to is that either the theories of reincarnation and Karma are false, since all data from psychology and history is against it, or we must make a leap of faith and say it operates in a "spiritual realm" and does not benefit mankind in any verifiable sense.

Inadequacies of the Law of Karma

Several other clear reasons demonstrate that the so-called "Law of Karma" itself is a myth. It simply does not exist except in the minds of reincarnationists. And it is not even a *good* myth, but rather a pernicious, evil concept which has caused untold human suffering and misery.

1. It has no scientific evidence to support it.

2. It has no analogy in nature. There is no illustration or example of it in the world in which we live.

3. Its infinite regression to past lives in order to explain everything which happens in the present robs history of any meaning. It assumes a cyclic view of history which denies that unique and final events take place in history. Everything is repeated endlessly with no final meaning. There is no beginning or climax to history.

4. It does not satisfy man's moral sensitivity or sense of justice.

5. It does not provide any absolute standards of right and wrong. Thus, its administration of suffering must be arbitrary and capricious.

6. It teaches that suffering is the only real purpose in life. Man has an innate aversion to such a theory.

7. Since it views each individual life as having no purpose outside of its own suffering, there is no concept of living for the glory of God or for the good of others. Hence, the Law of Karma is intrinsically selfish and self-centered.

8. It cripples the unity of humanity, since each soul is

trapped in a cycle of rebirths which benefits only that individual soul.

9. It produces despair, fatalism, pessimism, etc.

10. It cannot apply any ethical pressure to live a good life *now* as opposed to waiting until a later life.

11. It teaches that suffering is one's own fault, and that it can never ultimately come from the world or other people. It is a psychologically devastating concept.

12. It causes people to ignore the suffering of others.

13. It does not encourage people to alleviate human suffering.

14. It produces pride among the rich and healthy, and shame within the poor and sick.

15. It destroys all self-identity. Since "you" are "you" only in this life and "you" have actually been an endless number of people, and "you" will never know any or all of your past lives, "you" are a faceless nonperson with no self-identity. This is psychologically harmful.

16. It allows no place for forgiveness, since Karma can neither give nor recognize forgiveness. It gives no grace, exercises no mercy, displays no love. How can the Law of Karma be just, yet supposedly solve the problem of evil if it does not have grace, mercy, love, or forgiveness as an essential part of its nature or administration? The Law of Karma is cruel.

17. It does not answer the question, "If I sin as an *adult* in this life, how is it just to punish me as an *infant* in a future life?"

18. It makes unnecessary any repentance or restitution in this life for evil done in this life. According to some reincarnationists, the Law of Karma does not even allow expiation in this life for evil done in this life. Since you will have to pay your Karmic debt in a future life, nothing need be done. How can the Law of Karma be *just* if it makes repentance useless?

19. It does not demonstrate why it is not possible for someone else to suffer vicariously in your place and to pay off your Karmic debt for you.

20. Those who believe in the Law of Karma assume that all punishments for evil will be *finite*. They assume that there are no evils so great that the punishment for them will be infinite in duration and intensity.

Social Problems and Reincarnation

The theory of Karmic reincarnation is politically reactionary. It is a convenient tool of the rich upper classes for oppressing and exploiting the lower classes. It teaches the oppressed majority to accept their poverty and deprivation as punishment for past evils. The rich deserve the "good life" while the poor deserve their suffering. A consistent reincarnationist would never seek the overthrow of corrupt governments. The plight of the Untouchables in India reveals the political impact of the theory of reincarnation.

The theory of transmigration also leads to financial and ecological ruin. Because insects and animals may be Karmic rebirths of human souls, no attempt is made to destroy insects and rodents which eat food supplies. Thus, by allowing these marauders to eat tons of food, people are forced to die of starvation! Also, nothing is done to stop the spread of disease by insect infestation. Is it any wonder that disease as well as famine is a common experience in cultures where the theory of transmigration is accepted? It leads to human misery on a massive scale.

The Western world should take a long and probing look at the Eastern world and its human misery because such misery is a direct result of the embracing of Karmic reincarnation. Too many Westerners have embraced Eastern theology without accepting the life-style that the theory entails.

The caste system of India which locks an individual into a certain class and prohibits any movement from one caste to another is the sociological fruit of the theory of Karmic reincarnation. Just as Christianity produced Western democracy and compassionate capitalism, Karmic reincarnation produces the oppression of India's caste system.

Why, then, do Westerners assume that they can embrace the *root* of Karmic reincarnation and, at the same time, escape from experiencing the economical, sociological, and political *fruit* of Karmic reincarnation? To the Eastern mind it must seem that Westerners "play" with reincarnation and do not seriously practice it as it should be. The Westerners want to live off the fruit of *Christianity* but embrace the root of Karmic reincarnation. Their attempt to "have their cake and eat it too" will only end in spiritual ruin.

Conclusion

Serious doubts arise concerning the intellectual integrity and scientific validity of the theory of Karmic reincarnation. It does not explain the world in which we live. It is devastating to every level of human existence. Its arguments have been examined and found to be invalid. The life-style which arises out of a reincarnational world and life view leads to political, economic, and sociological disaster. It is rooted in the world of the occult which is clearly denounced in the Scriptures.

It cannot, therefore, be accepted as a valid theology, philosophy, or life-style. Only the Christian world and life view can provide a credible, consistent perspective of life in the here and now as well as life beyond the grave.

Chapter 4

The Christian Position

It is our firm conviction that true biblical Christianity is the only philosophy in the world within which one can live what he believes and believe what he lives. More than enough evidence can be drawn from every level of human thought and experience to demonstrate the validity and superiority of biblical Christianity.

Since we have elsewhere examined the ways in which Christianity answers the basic questions by which we can examine any system of thought, we will here give a simple overview of the Christian world and life view.[21]

There is but one true God eternally existing in three persons—the Father, the Son, and the Holy Spirit. God is infinite and personal. Christianity rejects any idea that "God" is an impersonal force, energy or mind.

The universe is not eternal. It is not a part of God or an extension of God's being or essence, but was created by Him. It is dependent upon its Creator for its very existence.

Man was created in God's moral image and likeness. He is distinct from the rest of the world. Man is not a part of God or destined to become God. He was created to live for the glory of God and the good of others. The Scriptures do not teach the pre-existence of human souls before birth.

Man was created in righteousness, holiness and knowledge, with a free will to choose a life of obedience to God's will or a life of disobedience. Man embraced the way of disobedience and has suffered the consequences ever since (Gen. 1-3).

The sinfulness of the human soul is described vividly in Rom. 3:10-18:

> There is none righteous, not even one; there is none who understands; there is none who seeks for God; all have turned aside, together they have become useless; there is none who does good, there is not even one.
>
> Their throat is an open grave, with their tongues they keep deceiving, the poison of asps is under their lips; whose mouth is full of cursing and bitterness; their feet are swift to shed blood, destruction and misery are in their paths, and the path of peace have they not known.
>
> There is no fear of God before their eyes.

Man's rebellion against God led him to invent false religions. Thus, the Apostle Paul exposes the true origin of all idolatrous religions in Rom. 1:18-25.

> For the wrath of God is revealed from heaven against all ungodliness and unrighteousness of men, who suppress the truth in unrighteousness, because that which is known about God is evident within them; for God made it evident to them. For since the creation of the world His invisible attributes, His eternal power and divine nature, have been clearly seen, being understood through what has been made, so that they are without excuse. For even though they knew God, they did not honor Him as God, nor give thanks; but they became futile in their speculations, and their foolish heart was darkened. Professing to be wise, they became fools, and exchanged the glory of the incorruptible God for an image in the form of corruptible man and of birds and four-footed animals and crawling creatures.
>
> Therefore God gave them over in the lusts of their hearts to impurity, that their bodies might be dishonored among them. For they exchanged the truth of God for a lie, and worshiped and served the creature rather than the Creator, who is blessed forever. Amen.

God's wrath against disobedience manifested itself in concrete historical events such as the Flood and the destruction of Sodom and Gomorrah. Why did God's wrath descend upon man?

> And the Lord saw that the wickedness of man was great on the earth and that every intent of the thoughts of his heart was only evil continually. (Gen. 6:5)
>
> The heart is deceitful above all things, and desperately wicked: who can know it? I the Lord search the heart, I try the reins, even to give every man according to his ways, and according to the fruit of his doings. (Jer. 17:9-10, KJV)

With sinful humanity forsaking God en masse, the only hope of salvation from the penalty, power and presence of sin was that God himself would take the initiative and provide eternal salvation for man. Since we could not and would not seek God, He had to seek us.

> And you were dead in your trespasses and sins, in which you formerly walked according to the course of this world according to the prince of the power of the air, of the spirit that is now working in the sons of disobedience. Among them we too all formerly lived in the lusts of our flesh, indulging the desires of the flesh and of the mind, and were by nature children of wrath, even as the rest. But God, being rich in mercy, because of His great love with which He loved us, even when we were dead in our transgressions, made us alive together with Christ (by grace you have been saved), and raised us up with Him, and seated us with Him in the heavenly places, in Christ Jesus. For by grace you have been saved through faith; and that not of yourselves, it is the gift of God; not as a result of works, that no one should boast. For we are His workmanship, created in Christ Jesus for good works, which God prepared beforehand, that we should walk in them. (Eph. 2:1-10)
>
> For while we were still helpless, at the right time Christ died for the ungodly. For one will hardly die for a righteous man; though perhaps for the good man someone would dare even to die. But God demonstrates His own love toward us, in that while we were yet sinners, Christ died for us. Much more then, having now been justified by His blood, we shall be saved from the wrath of God through Him! For if while we

were enemies, we were reconciled to God through the death of His Son, much more, having been reconciled, we shall be saved by His life. And not only this, but we also exult in God through our Lord Jesus Christ, through whom we have now received the reconciliation. (Rom. 5:6-11)

For God so loved the world, that He gave His only begotten Son, that whoever believes in Him should not perish, but have eternal life. For God did not send the Son into the world to judge the world; but that the world should be saved through Him. He who believes in Him is not judged; he who does not believe has been judged already, because he has not believed in the name of the only begotten Son of God. And this is the judgment, that the light is come into the world, and men loved the darkness rather than the light; for their deeds were evil. For everyone who does evil hates the light, and does not come to the light, lest his deeds should be exposed. But he who practices the truth comes to the light, that his deeds may be manifested as having been wrought in God. (John 3:16-21)

Thus, even though "the wages of sin is death" (Rom. 6:23), "the Father has sent the Son to be the Savior of the world" (1 John 4:14).

But, how could God's plan of salvation work? How could the debt of our sin be paid? Since we could not pay off our own debt, who would show mercy, love and grace and provide forgiveness for us?

The Christian answer is that Jesus Christ, who is God the Son, the second person of the Triune Godhead, actually died in the place of sinners and paid the full debt of their sin by His infinite suffering. He had no sin of His own, and thus could suffer in our place. He died the death we should have died just as He lived the life we should have lived.

The ancient Hebrew prophets described in graphic detail how the Messiah would suffer in our place. Isaiah's language is matchless in its description of how Christ would pay our "Karmic debt."

Who hath believed our report? and to whom is the arm of the Lord revealed?

For he shall grow up before him as a tender plant, and as a

root out of a dry ground: he hath no form nor comeliness; and when we shall see him, there is no beauty that we should desire him.

He is despised and rejected of men; a man of sorrows, and acquainted with grief: and we hid as it were our faces from him; he was despised, and we esteemed him not.

Surely he hath borne our griefs, and carried our sorrows: yet we did esteem him stricken, *smitten of God*, and *afflicted. But he was wounded for our transgressions, he was bruised for our iniquities: the chastisement of our peace was upon him; and with his stripes we are healed.* All we like sheep have gone astray; we have turned every one to his own way; and *the Lord hath laid on him the iniquity of us all.* He was oppressed, and he was afflicted, yet he opened not his mouth; he is brought as a lamb to the slaughter, and as a sheep before her shearers is dumb, so he openeth not his mouth. He was taken from prison and from judgment: and who shall declare his generation? for he was cut off out of the land of the living: *for the transgression of my people was he stricken.* And he made his grave with the wicked, and with the rich in his death; because he had done no violence, neither was any deceit in his mouth.

Yet it pleased the Lord to bruise him; he hath put him to grief: when thou shalt make *his soul an offering for sin*, he shall see his seed, he shall prolong his days, and the pleasure of the Lord shall prosper in his hand. He shall see of the travail of his soul, and shall be satisfied: by his knowledge shall my righteous servant justify many; *for he shall bear their iniquities.* Therefore will I divide him a portion with the great, and he shall divide the spoil with the strong; because he hath poured out his soul unto death: and he was numbered with the transgressors; and *he bore the sin of many*, and made intercession for the transgressors. (Isa. 53, KJV)

The New Testament affirms that Jesus of Nazareth was indeed the long-awaited Messiah. He suffered and died for our sins in order that we might be saved from the consequences of our sins.

For I delivered to you as of first importance what I also received, that Christ died for our sins according to the Scriptures, and that He was buried, and that He was raised on the third day according to the Scriptures. (1 Cor. 15:3-4)

> For Christ did not enter a holy place made with hands, a mere copy of the true one, but into heaven itself, now to appear in the presence of God for us; nor was it that He should offer Himself often, as the high priest enters the holy place year by year with blood not his own. Otherwise, He would have needed to suffer often since the foundation of the world; but now once at the consummation He has been manifested to put away sin by the sacrifice of Himself. And inasmuch as it is appointed for men to die once, and after this comes judgment; so Christ also, having been offered once to bear the sins of many, shall appear a second time, not to bear sin, to those who eagerly await Him, for salvation. (Heb. 9:24-28)
>
> He made Him who knew no sin to be sin on our behalf, that we might become the righteousness of God in Him. (2 Cor. 5:21)

Did Jesus Christ pay off the *full* debt of our sin and thus make unnecessary any cyclic rebirths?

One of Christ's seven last statements on the cross is recorded in John 19:30. It has been traditionally translated into English as, "It is finished."

The Greek word which is found in the text was not fully understood until recent archaeological discoveries in the Middle East. It was discovered that the word which had been translated "finished" was actually a common word in the first century that was stamped on a bill of sale when that bill was *paid in full*. Thus, modern commentators and translators agree that what Jesus cried from the cross should be translated, "It has been paid in full."

Christ "paid in full" all that we owed to divine justice. Thus, salvation is now declared a *free gift* given to all who believe in Christ (Rom. 6:23).

The work of Christ in paying off our debt to God resulted in His right and power to purge us from all sin. Thus, the Gospel of Christ is the good news that Jesus Christ has done all that is necessary for our salvation. His sacrifice and suffering have completely satisfied all that God's law required.[22]

> God, who at sundry times and in divers manners spake in

time past unto the fathers by the prophets, hath in these last days spoken unto us by his Son, whom he hath appointed heir of all things, by whom also he made the worlds; who being the brightness of his glory, and the express image of his person, and upholding all things by the word of his power, *when he had by himself purged our sins*, sat down on the right hand of the Majesty on high. (Heb. 1:1-3, KJV)

By the which will we are *sanctified*, through the offering of the body of Jesus Christ *once for all*. And every priest standeth daily ministering and offering often times the same sacrifices, which can never take away sins: but this man, after he had offered *one sacrifice for sins for ever*, sat down on the right hand of God; from henceforth expecting till his enemies be made his footstool. For *by one offering he hath perfected for ever them that are sanctified*. (Heb. 10:10-14, KJV)

According to the Gospel, Christ purged us from all our sins on the cross. Thus, there is no *need* for anyone to purge himself by his own suffering in life-after-life-after-life.

Is it any wonder that in the Western world, once the Gospel of God's love in Christ Jesus gained a hearing, it supplanted the theory of Karmic reincarnation? It is obvious why the Gospel of love and forgiveness triumphed over a hard and cruel Law of Karmic rebirths. It is reasonable to believe that whenever biblical Christianity is objectively compared to all the Eastern and Western reincarnational religions, it will shine forth as the only valid faith.

This possibly explains the modern problem. Most Western people turning to the theory of reincarnation do not evidence any acquaintance with or knowledge of biblical Christianity. The "Christianity" from which they turn is, in reality, the secularized humanistic liberalism and neo-orthodoxy of many of the mainline churches. Secularism, liberalism and neo-orthodox theologies are not "Christian" but humanistic religions which have their origin in scientism and rationalism.[23] Thus, because these people do not understand biblical Christianity, they assume that "Christianity" cannot answer their intellectual questions, or the desires of their hearts. They turn away from a secularized religion with their hearts and minds empty.

We are convinced, however, by experience and by sound reason that when true orthodox biblical Christianity is examined with an open heart and mind, it evidences itself to be superior to all other beliefs.

Without Jesus Christ, there is no way to approach the Father, no way to learn the truth about the Father, and no way to live with the Father (John 14:6). Christ is the only mediator between God and man (1 Tim. 2:5). Faith must rest in the Lord Jesus Christ, who triumphed over sin and death and now lives in His resurrected human body.

God has revealed that "it is appointed for men to die *once*, and after this comes judgment" (Heb. 9:27). At death, a believer in Christ goes immediately in his spirit to be with Christ in heaven (Phil. 1:21-23; 2 Cor. 5:6-8). He looks forward to a future resurrection of his body, not a reincarnation into some other body. Without the assurance of resurrection, the Christian's outlook would be as doleful as the reincarnationist's. The Christian hope of a bodily resurrection excludes any possibility of a soul having more than one body, and is the final answer to the riddle of reincarnation.

---

21. Morey, R., *A Christian's Handbook for Defending the Faith*, Pres. & Ref. Pub. Co., Nutley, N.J., 1979.

22. See: *The Saving Work of Christ*, where the necessity and nature of the atonement is demonstrated.

23. Machen, G., *Christianity and Liberalism*, Wm. B. Eerdmans Publ. Co., Grand Rapids, Mich., 1974.

Appendix I

Objections and Answers

1. *Objection*. "No one can say that the world's total population has increased. Therefore any argument based on a supposed population growth is ungrounded and, hence, unacceptable."[24]

   Answer: The fact that some reincarnationists deny the increase of human population reveals the weight of the population argument and the desperate lengths to which they are forced to go to deny it.

   Evidence gathered by the United Nations Statistical Office is published in a yearly *Demographic Yearbook* which is available in any large library. It shows from year-to-year the rate of increase in the total world population. Even a brief survey of these materials lays to rest the reincarnationists' objections.

   According to McEvedz and Jones, *Atlas of World Population History* (Penguin Books, N.Y., 1978, p. 350), the growth of the population has been as follows:

A.D. 1575	500 million
1825	1 billion
1925	2 billion
1975	Almost 4 billion

Such evidence for the increase in the world's population is overwhelming.[25] We have yet to see any careful scientific refutation of this evidence by the reincarnationists.

Also, the Western reincarnational theories logically imply a *decrease* in world population. Even if the world population remained the same, how would this account for all the souls who are perfected through Karmic suffering, and escape the cycles of rebirths and are hence absorbed back into "being"?

2. *Objection*: "Reincarnation does not teach that people can become animals in a next life. Reincarnation is evolutionary in that it is the vehicle for the progressive perfection of mankind."

   Answer: The orthodox reincarnationists *do* teach that a human soul may be reborn into an animal body. See Johnson, J., *The Path of the Masters*, Sawan Service League, Panjob, India.

   It is true that this is denied by some Western reincarnationists. Why? Because they wish to make reincarnation palatable to the Western Christian public. But let it not be forgotten that a westernized "Christianized" theory of reincarnation is a deviation from the original theory.

3. *Objection*: "Reincarnation is not occult; it is scientific and is unrelated to the occult arts."

   Answer: You will find the Ouija board used in Holzer, H., *Born Again*, Doubleday & Co., Inc., N.Y., 1976, p. 73 ff. The use of spiritistic and occult means to "prove" reincarnation is found in nearly all of the writings of popular reincarnationists. Edgar Cayce was a self-admitted medium through whom "spirits" spoke. In J. Stearn's writings we find the use of astrology, mediums, spirit-guides, etc.[26] Without the use of occultic automatic writing, there would not be any books by Ruth Montgomery on the market.[27]

Make no mistake about it, reincarnation is occult and satanic to the core!

4. *Objection*: "Reincarnation is not hostile to Christianity. Many who believe in Christianity find no conflict or contradiction in accepting the theory of reincarnation."

Answer: Reincarnation conflicts with every essential truth of historic biblical Christianity. Cayce denied the trinity.[28] Ruth Montgomery denied the bodily resurrection of Christ.[29] Steiger and Williams deny the creation of the universe *ex nihilo*, and advocate pantheism.[30] They also deny the existence of evil.[31] The uniqueness and deity of Christ is denied in Stearn's book, *The Search for a Soul*, on p. 155. All the reincarnationists blatantly deny the eternal conscious punishment of the wicked in hell, and the Christian's hope of heaven.

Those who hold to reincarnational theories are invariably hostile to orthodox biblical Christianity.

24. See: Cooper, L. S., *Reincarnation*, Theosophical Press, Wheaton, Ill., 1959, p. IX.

25. See also: Fitz & Lefzer, *World Population*, The University of Chicago Press, Chicago, 1968.

26. Stearn, J., *The Search for a Soul*, Doubleday & Co., Inc., N.Y., 1973, p. 152, etc.

_____, *The Matter of Immortality*, Atheniun, N.Y., 1976.

27. Montgomery, R., *Here and Hereafter*, Coward-McCann & Georghegan, Inc., N.Y., 1968.

_____, *A World Beyond*, Coward, McCann & Georghegan, Inc., N.Y., 1974.

_____, *Companions Along the Way*, Coward, McCann & Georghegan, Inc., N.Y., 1974.

28. Swihart, ibid., pp. 12-20.

29. Montgomery, R., *Companions Along the Way*, p. 133.

30. Steiger, B., & Williams, L., *Other Lives*, Hawthorn Books, Inc., N.Y., 1969, p. 128.

31. Ibid.

Appendix II

The reincarnational books referred to in this study are not recommended reading as they are filled with historical distortions and misleading statements. Nevertheless, the following bibliography lists the source materials which were consulted in the course of research into the theory of reincarnation.

Cerminana, G., *Many Lives, Many Loves*, Wm. Sloane Ass'n, N.Y., 1963.

————, *Many Mansions*, William Morrow & Co., N.Y., 1950.

Cooper, L. S., *Reincarnation*, Theosophical Press, Wheaton, Ill., 1959.

Head, J. and Cranston, S., *Reincarnation in World Thought*, Julian Press, N.Y., 1967.

————, *Reincarnation: An East-West Anthology*, The Theosophical Pub. House, Wheaton, Ill., 1961.

Holzer, H., *Born Again*, Doubleday & Co., N.Y., 1967.

Johnson, J., *The Path of the Masters*, Sawan Service League, Panjob, India.

Langley, N., *Edgar Cayce on Reincarnation*, Castle Books, N.Y., 1967.

Montgomery, R., *Here and Hereafter*, Coward-McCann, N.Y., 1968.

————, *A World Beyond*, Coward, McCann & Georghegan, N.Y., 1971.

————, *Companions Along the Way*, Coward, McCann & Georghegan, N.Y., 1974.

Stearn, J., *The Search for a Soul*, Doubleday & Co., N.Y., 1973.

————, *A Matter of Immortality*, Atheneun, N.Y., 1976.

Steiger, B., & Williams, C., *Other Lives*, Hawthorn Books, N.Y., 1969.

Surgrue, T., *There Is a River*, Dell Pub. Co., N.Y., 1960.

"The Edgar Cayce Legacy," A.R.E., Inc., Virginia Beach, Virginia.

Westerhead, L. D., "The Case for Reincarnation," M. C. Pero., Surrey, England, 1958.

Walker, E. D., *Reincarnation*, University Books, N.Y., 1965.

Bibliography

Carnell, E. J., *Christian Commitment*, The Macmillan Co., New York, 1957.

Clark, G. H., *A Christian View of Men and Things*, Wm. B. Eerdmans Pub. Co., Grand Rapids, 1967.

————, *Religion, Reason and Revelation*, The Craig Press, New Jersey, 1978.

————, *The Philosophy of Science and Belief in God*, The Craig Press, New Jersey, 1964.

Chang, Lit Sen, *Zen-Existentialism*, Pres. & Ref. Pub. Co., N.J., 1969.

Guinness, Os., *The Dust of Death*, I.V.P., 1978.

Lewis, C. S., *Mere Christianity*, The Macmillan Co., New York, 1966.

————, *Miracles*, The Macmillan Co., New York, 1966.

Machen, G., *Christianity and Liberalism*, Wm. B. Eerdmans Pub. Co., Grand Rapids, 1974.

————, *The Origin of Paul's Religion*, Wm. B. Eerdmans Pub. Co., Grand Rapids, 1965.

McDowell, J., *Evidence That Demands a Verdict*, Campus Crusade for Christ, Inc., 1972.

Morey, R. A., *A Christian's Handbook for Defending the Faith*, Pres. & Ref. Pub. Co., N.J., 1979.

————, *The Saving Work of Christ*, G. A. M., Sterling, Va., 1980.

Orr, J. E., *Faith That Makes Sense*, The Judson Press, Valley Forge, 1965.

Schaeffer, F., *Escape from Reason*, I.V.P., Illinois, 1968.

————, *He Is There and Is Not Silent*, Tyndale House Pub., Ill. 1972.

————, *How Then Should We Live?*, Fleming H. Revell Co., N.J., 1976.

————, *Genesis in Space and Time*, I.V.P., Illinois, 1972.

Short, A. R., *Why Believe?*, I.V.P., London, 1962.

Sproul, R. C., *If There Is a God, Why Are There Atheists?* Bethany Fellowship, Inc., Minn., 1974.

Van Til, C., *A Christian Theory of Knowledge*, Pres. & Ref. Pub. Co., N.J., 1969.

————, *The Defense of the Faith*, Pres. & Ref. Pub. Co., Phila., 1963.